HITLER'S BOLD CHALLENGERS

EUROPEAN HISTORY BOOKS
CHILDREN'S EUROPEAN HISTORY

Speedy Publishing LLC

40 E. Main St. #1156

Newark, DE 19711

www.speedypublishing.com

Copyright 2017

A dolf Hitler led the Axis powers in World War II as they attempted to conquer the world. Who stood against him? Let's find out!

GREATER EAST ASIA CONFERENCE

A GLOBAL WAR

From 1939 to 1945 three countries tried to dominate and defeat the rest of the world. Known together as the Axis powers, Germany, Italy, and Japan caused a war that disrupted the world and caused millions of deaths.

The Axis was led by Germany's Adolf Hitler. He had developed two theories: that white people were naturally superior to people of all other colors, and that the German "race" should dominate all the other people in Europe. He convinced many in Germany that all their problems were due to bad actions by "lesser peoples" like Jews, Africans, and Arabs. He then took the great German war machine into battle against the nations of Europe.

ADOLF HITLER

ADOLF HITLER DURING HIS SPEECH TO THE REICHSTAG (1939)

The countries lined up against the Axis and were led by Great Britain, France, the United States, China, and, eventually, the Soviet Union. Let's see who their leaders were.

GREAT BRITAIN: WINSTON CHURCHILL

Winston Spencer Churchill, part of a famed British political and military family, was born in 1874. He joined the military as a young man and served in India and in the Second Boer War in South Africa. He was captured and managed to escape, then traveled over three hundred miles to British lines. This made him a hero in British eyes.

WINSTON CHURCHILL, 26 YEARS OLD

WINSTON CHURCHILL

Churchill was a gifted writer, and added to his fame with books and articles on many topics. He first was elected to Parliament in 1900. For the next thirty years he held many posts in government, including heading the Navy during World War I.

However, in the 1930s Churchill fell out of favor. He was ridiculed as a has-been. But, he persisted as a back-bench member of Parliament, and turned out many books and articles during his time "in the wilderness". He became an expert on the threat that Germany was becoming during the 1930s, and warned of the threat even when most people did not want to think about the need for another war.

WINSTON CHURCHILL

WINSTON CHURCHILL REVIEWS AN
HONOR GUARD OF THE ROYAL NAVY

At the start of World War II in 1939, Churchill again became head of the British Navy. He disagreed strongly with the Prime Minister, Neville Chamberlain, who wanted to try to find a peaceful solution to Hitler's ambitions.

Finally, in the face of war and Hitler's growing success, Chamberlain resigned and Churchill took his place. Soon after, Germany invaded and defeated France. Great Britain was left as the last major power in Europe opposing the Axis.

BRITISH PRIME MINISTER WINSTON CHURCHILL IS
GREETED BY FIELD MARSHALL BERNARD MONTGOMERY

HEINKEL HE 111 BOMBERS
DURING THE BATTLE OF BRITAIN

C hurchill rallied the country with a never-surrender attitude, even though it was not clear Great Britain could survive a threatened German invasion. Fortunately, British fighter planes were able to gain control of the skies over the English Channel from Germany in "The Battle of Britain". Hitler turned his forces toward a surprise attack on the Soviet Union.

Churchill led Great Britain through six years of war through the liberation of all the countries Germany, Japan and Italy had conquered, to the surrender of Germany in May, and Japan in September of 1945. After the war he wrote a five-volume history that is one of the great records of that time. He won the Nobel Prize for literature for his military writings.

L TO R: BRITISH PRIME MINISTER WINSTON CHURCHILL, PRESIDENT HARRY S. TRUMAN, AND SOVIET LEADER JOSEF STALIN

Churchill continued to be a force in British politics for many years, and finally died in 1965. He accomplished great things in many fields during his life even though his health was never good. In fact his greatest triumph during World War II took place when many had thought he was a has-been whose career was over.

CHURCHILL QUOTES

Winston Churchill had a gift with words, even though he struggled with a stutter in public speaking. Here are some of his famous statements:

- Of the failed attempts to avoid war with the Axis: "You were given the choice between war and dishonor. You chose dishonor, and you will have war."

He also said, "An appeaser is one who feeds a crocodile, hoping it will eat him last."

During his first speech as Prime Minister, he explained what he could do: "I have nothing to offer but blood, toil, tears, and sweat."

YALTA CONFERENCE
(CHURCHILL, ROOSEVELT, STALIN)

WINSTON CHURCHILL AT
A BBC MICROPHONE

Praising the pilots of the Royal Air Force who won the Battle of Britain, he said, "Never in the field of human conflict was so much owed by so many to so few."

WINSTON CHURCHILL WITH ROYAL
AIR FORCE BOMBER COMMAND

CHARLES DE GAULLE

FRANCE: CHARLES DE GAULLE

Charlese de Gaulle was born in 1890 and died in 1970. In World War I, 1914-18, he was a French soldier against Germany. He was wounded and captured, and tried to escape five times.

After the French victory in World War I de Gaulle continued in the military and rose through the ranks. He developed theories for conducting modern warfare which, unfortunately, his superiors did not adopt. De Gaulle's tactics would have had far greater success against the German attack in World War II.

CHARLES DE GAULLE
ACCOMPANIED BY GENERAL MAST

WINSTON CHURCHILL AND GENERAL CHARLES DE GAULLE

In 1939, de Gaulle became a general. As the Germans overran the French positions and France got ready to surrender, de Gaulle escaped to Great Britain. There he set up the "Free French" government to continue the war. De Gaulle inspired French exiles to fight on the side of the Allies, along with Resistance fighters within France.

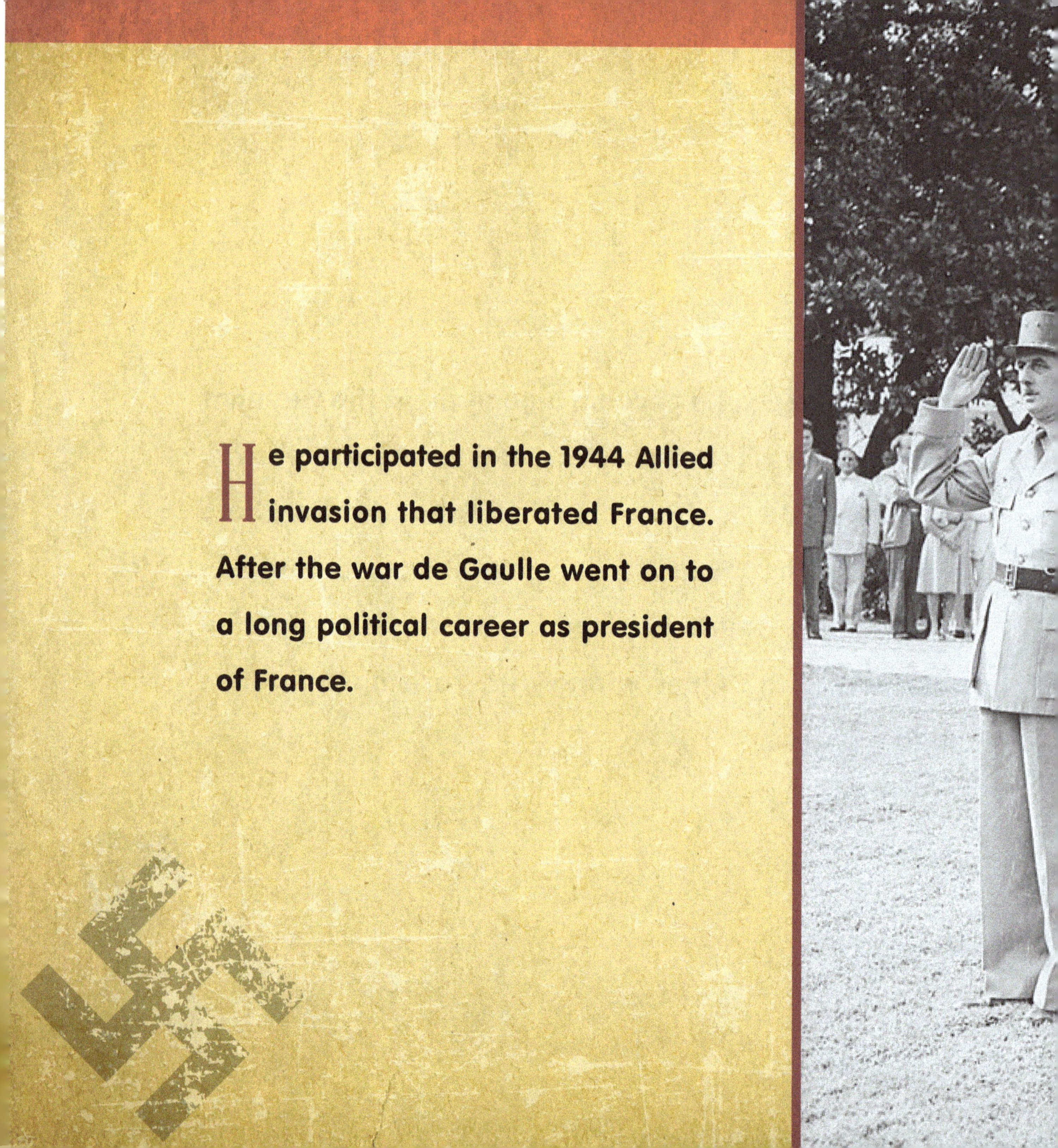

He participated in the 1944 Allied invasion that liberated France. After the war de Gaulle went on to a long political career as president of France.

PRESIDENT CHARLES DE GAULLE DURING
WELCOMING CEREMONIES ON THE WHITE HOUSE

CHARLES DE GAULLE DURING A PARADE IN FRANCE

DE GAULLE QUOTES

De Gaulle had an ironic turn of phrase. Some of his famous quotes include:

- "The better I get to know men, the more I find myself loving dogs."

- Of the challenge of leading France: "How can you govern a country that has 246 kinds of cheese?"

- "I have come to the conclusion that politics are too serious a matter to be left to the politicians."

UNITED STATES: FRANKLIN DELANO ROOSEVELT

Franklin D. Roosevelt was born in 1882. He served as President of the United States from 1933 until his death in 1945, longer by far than any other president. Roosevelt came from a powerful New York family and rose quickly in politics. However, he became ill with polio and spent years battling the illness.

FRANKLIN DELANO ROOSEVELT WITH
FATHER JAMES ROOSEVELT IN 1895

GOVERNOR FRANKLIN DELANO ROOSEVELT

Having recovered enough that he could walk a few steps on his own, Roosevelt became Governor of New York in 1929, and then was elected President in the 1932 election.

Roosevelt led the country through recovery from the Great Depression that had started in 1929 and brought in many social programs that many Americans now take for granted like Social Security. However, his greatest role was as Commander in Chief during the Second World War.

FRANKLIN D. ROOSEVELT, CHURCHILL, M. KING, AND SEVERAL MILITARY PERSONEL IN QUEBEC

AMERICAN MILITARY OFFICIALS IN EUROPE.

When the war started in 1939, the United States was neutral. However, Roosevelt made many arrangements to support Great Britain in its fight against Germany. Once Japan attacked the United States in 1941 and Germany declared war on the U.S., Roosevelt unleashed the country's forces in a war in both Europe and the Pacific.

Roosevelt is considered one of the greatest presidents of the United States. He projected optimism and hope in dark times. One of his most famous quotes is, "The only thing we have to fear is fear itself."

THE ALLIED LEADERS OF THE
ASIAN AND PACIFIC THEATRE

JOSEF STALIN, 1902

SOVIET UNION: JOSEF STALIN

J osef Stalin was born in 1878, became leader of the Soviet Union in 1924, and ruled the country until his death in 1953. He was a strong leader during the war, first on the side of Germany against Poland, and then defending the Soviet Union against a German invasion.

However, he was also the author of monstrous crimes that led to the deaths of millions of his fellow countrymen.

Learn more about him in the Baby Professor book Who Was Josef Stalin?

CHIANG KAI-SHEK

CHINA: CHIANG KAI-SHEK

Chiang Kai-shek (1887-1975) led the Republic of China from 1928. At the end of World War II, after the defeat of Japan, the republican government was itself defeated by the Communist Party's Red Army. Chiang contnued to lead the Republic of China on the island of Taiwan until 1950. For much of his tenure China and Japan were at war on Chinese territory, and Chiang's government could not find a way to make common cause with the communists even against the Japanese.

CHIANG KAI-SHEK QUOTES

Chiang had a strong sense of duty and faith. Here are two of his famous statements:

- "Only a fighting nation can make itself responsible for world peace."

- "Prayer is more than meditation. In meditation the source of strength is one's self. When one prays, he goes to a source of strength greater than his own."

VICTORY NEEDED TEAMWORK

It was not just the leaders who won the victory! Millions of people around the world joined together to turn back the Axis threat. People fought on the front lines, in ships, and in planes. At home they assembled tanks and ammunition, grew food for the troops, nursed the wounded, or worked to break the codes the enemies used to communicate.

It always takes a team to defeat a huge threat. Learn more about the teamwork of World War II in Baby Professor books like The Brave Women of World War II, The Theaters of World War II: Europe and the Pacific, and The 4-Day Battle of Midway.